We Found a Hound

By Cameron Macintosh

Jude and Mum were out walking in the town.

They sat down in the park to have a snack.

A brown dog came up to them.

"Wow, you are a cute hound!" said Mum.

"He does not have a name tag," said Jude.

"Let's play for a while,"
said Mum.
"Maybe the hound's mum or dad
will come for him."

Jude and Mum played at the park for a long time.

But no one came for the hound.

"We will take him back
to the house," said Mum.

"We can help him find his mum
or dad," said Jude.

Back at Jude's house, the hound did a big howl.

"How will we find his mum or dad?" said Jude.

"Let's put a card up in town," said Mum.

Jude put a photo of the hound on a big pole.

Soon, Mum's phone rang.

"My name is Jeff," said a man.
"You have found my hound!
His name is Rowdy."

Mum and Jude walked Rowdy back to the park.

Rowdy ran to Jeff at once.

"Thank you very much!" said Jeff.
"I was so upset about Rowdy.
He got out of my yard."

Jude was sad to see Rowdy go, but he was glad the hound was safe and happy.

CHECKING FOR MEANING

1. Where did Jude and Mum find the hound? *(Literal)*

2. What was the hound's name? *(Literal)*

3. What might Mum and Jude have done if they didn't find Rowdy's owner? *(Inferential)*

EXTENDING VOCABULARY

hound	What does *hound* mean? What is another word the author could have used for *hound*?
howl	What does a *howl* sound like? How was Rowdy feeling if he was howling? What other noises can dogs make?
Rowdy	*Rowdy* is the dog's name in this book. What does the word *rowdy* mean? Do you think it's a good name for a dog?

MOVING BEYOND THE TEXT

1. Have you ever lost something? How did you find it?

2. What other animals howl, besides dogs?

3. Have you ever been lost? How did it feel?

4. What are some things you should and should not do if you get lost?

DIPHTHONGS

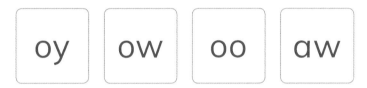

| oy | ow | oo | aw |

PRACTICE WORDS

out

town

down

brown

hound

house

sound

howl

Rowdy

How

found

Wow

hound's